Bedtime Stories for Kids

Relaxing Stories for Children's Bedtime

Imogen Young

© Copyright 2021 - All rights reserved.

The content contained within this book may not be reproduced, duplicated or transmitted without direct written permission from the author or the publisher.
Under no circumstances will any blame or legal responsibility be held against the publisher, or author, for any damages, reparation, or monetary loss due to the information contained within this book. Either directly or indirectly.

Legal Notice:
This book is copyright protected. This book is only for personal use. You cannot amend, distribute, sell, use, quote or paraphrase any part, or the content within this book, without the consent of the author or publisher.

Disclaimer Notice:
Please note the information contained within this document is for educational and entertainment purposes only. All effort has been executed to present accurate, up to date, and reliable, complete information. No warranties of any kind are declared or implied. Readers acknowledge that the author is not engaging in the rendering of legal, financial, medical or professional advice. The content within this book has been derived from various sources. Please consult a licensed professional before attempting any techniques outlined in this book.

By reading this document, the reader agrees that under no circumstances is the author responsible for any losses, direct or indirect, which are incurred as a result of the use of information contained within this document, including, but not limited to, — errors, omissions, or inaccuracies.

Table of Contents

Deep into Mexico's Country 6
Animals 19
His Spade 33
Unicorns 42
The Poodle and the Donkey 46
The Black and White Kitten 49
Mr. West 53
Say Please 72
The Raven and the Crow 85
Alligators 98

Deep into Mexico's Country

A long time ago, high up on a mountain, deep into Mexico's country, there lived a very beautiful Monarch Butterfly called Marina. She lived in the little town of Acuna and was very popular with everyone in town. You see, she had a very special gift. She was a magic monarch! Everyone in town knew of her special powers, and many came to her for help when they needed something special done, like a sick family member or a lost child.

Acuna was a happy town. There were no arguments or fights, no quarrels at all. The people of Acuna who had never ventured outside of the city limits did not know of the world war. They did not need to know the word because never had there been one, and never would there be one anywhere near Acuna. Acuna was a perfectly tranquil place. Everyone was very polite, and the men always held a door open for a lady to pass through first. Everyone went to church on Sunday mornings, and everyone liked their neighbors. Acuna was simply a most beautiful town, and for some reason, it always had been.

As it happened, Marina was also the town's school teacher, so she was very close to all the children in town. On holiday weekends, Marina taught classes in togetherness at the town hall. These classes were loved by all who had ever attended them because she used her magic to teach her class. What this meant was that the people who came to her classes learned something that only she knew. What she showed them was not available anywhere else in the world. Not in the capitol of Mexico, not in the United States capitol, and nowhere in Europe would you ever find out about what she knew.

Little Pepita had heard about the classes but had been told that she was too young to go yet, and always heard her Mommy and Daddy say, "Maybe next year my little squash seed, maybe next year we will take you with us!"

Pepita was a baby when the classes first began, but she had heard about them and wanted to go with her parents every year when Cinco de Mayo came around again. Alas, she was always too young. Pepita lived next door to a dress shop.

Every Wednesday morning, the shopkeeper would put a brand new and beautiful dress in the shop window for all the townspeople to see. And every Wednesday morning, Pepita would be there, out on the sidewalk, waiting to see what the shopkeeper would be putting out today. This Wednesday, she gasped when she saw the new dress. It was the most beautiful dress she had ever seen. It was pure white, with bands of ribbon sewed around it. There were three just below the shoulders, and five bands down around the hips. The bands were red, green, gold, and orange, and they glistened in the sun as she stared at them. Pepita wanted that dress so badly. She was just a kid, and although she thought about this, she could not find a way to buy that dress.

Later that night, lying on her bed, she thought something up. She thought that if she had something that somebody else wanted, she could sell that something to them and then go and buy her dream dress. "Oh," Pepita said, "I want that dress so badly, I must have it!" With that, little Pepita fell asleep.

It was April, and the sun shone brightly across the gleaming tiles in the town square. Everyone was going about their business as usual, and everyone was happy. For one thing, there was a big annual celebration coming up next month, and this meant folks were making plans, buying goods to cook special holiday foods, and checking out there dancing clothes, because they all knew it would soon be Cinco de Mayo, and that meant good food, good cheer and lots of dancing in the streets of the little town of Acuna.

When little Pepita learned that the grand celebration was getting nearer, she jumped up and ran to her Momma to ask the big question yet. Why just last night, she had realized that indeed, she was now a year older and maybe, just maybe, she would get to go to the Cinco de Mayo celebration and attend the great Marina's class. Oh, how she wanted to go to that class.

She found her Mommy in the kitchen, making tortillas, and burst into the room much too quickly. Her Mommy jumped out of the way just in time because she was carrying a very hot plate and did not want to drop it on little Pepita. "Why are you running about the house at top speed, little one?" she asked Pepita. "I just found out that next month is going to be Cinco de Mayo again, so can I go this time, Mommy, can I, can it?" she pleaded. "Come here, Pepita, and calm down." Her Mommy told her. "Now, I thought that this time..." At these words, little Pepita launched into her Moms arms. "Hold on, child, you don't even know what I was going to say yet!" she exclaimed.

"Yes, I do," Pepita claimed, "you were going to say that I can go!" Pepita said much too loudly. "Well, you do take the surprise out of everything now, don't you little one?" her Mom said as Pepita started bouncing and dancing all over the kitchen. "Yaaay! I'm going to Cinco... I'm going to Cinco," little Pepita sang. All her Mommy could do was to smile a huge smile and try to reach out to hug her little girl who was moving around much too quickly for that to happen. "Stand st ill for a moment, and let me give you a hug." Her Mommy told Pepita.

As it was a Tuesday afternoon, Pepita made plans to go down to the dress shop the next day as it was "change the display" day, and she would get to see a new dress. This she did, and it was as beautiful as she had hoped for. Like the other one, but the bands had only red and green colors around the dress. Still, she loved it and was beginning to think that something was going to happen to buy a new dress.

The days and weeks in Acuna passed, and the town was transformed into a happy and colorful fiesta town, ready for the coming Cinco holiday weekend. Pepita walked along the sidewalk in town and marveled at all the colors of the banners that were waving in the wind up on their poles, up and down the street. She smelled fresh-baked pies and barbeque, and oh my goodness, she was getting so excited. She had waited all of her little life for this day, and it was soon to be here.

Then, she noticed on her calendar that she was actually in the week before Cinco de Mayo. Suddenly she had almost forgotten about the dress she wanted so badly but instead began to think about how to prepare for the big class she had always dreamed of attending. The time was very close. She got all her school supplies ready, a notebook, some lined paper to go in it, pencils and a pencil sharpener, and ready.

When that Sunday morning came, Pepita and her Mommy and Daddy went to the celebration together. There was music and dancing and lots of great food laid out on a long table. It was simply Grande!

Then, the music stopped, and Marina took to the stage and spoke into the microphone. "As Master of Ceremony this year, it is my honor to invite you all to my annual Cinco de Mayo class at the church in one hour," She announced.

This got little Pepita very excited, and she started to jump up and down right there in one spot. A little boy noticed this and walked over to her. "Hi, my name is Pablo. What's yours?" he said. Lots of people noticed this and especially Pepita's Mommy and Daddy. There were smiles and lots of Oooh's and Aaah's before

Pepita answered the boy. "My name is Pepita!" she said with a sweet smile. "Would you like to sit with me in the class?" Pablo asked Pepita.

Well, little Pepita looked up to her parents for approval, and they both nodded yes, and told Pablo to join them so they could all be together for such a great event. Pablo said, "let me go ask my Dad," and ran off across the square. Before long, Pablo came running back with a happy gait and exclaimed in joy, "it's okay with my Dad, so I would be happy to sit with you at the class." And with that, it was settled.

When the time came, everyone lined up to get into the big old church and found their seats. There were hymns and a sermon by the pastor and then the class.

The beautiful Monarch Butterfly called Marina stood tall up at the podium and began to speak. It was as though the air in the church began to crackle, and no one spoke a word in anticipation of what the Monarch would teach them. Unknown to the little ones, most of the townspeople already knew what this class was about but needed a refresher because, they thought, you can never get enough of one of the best things on Earth. Mindfulness!

"In a child's life," Marina began, "everything is simple and blissful because they do not know any other way." Marina hesitated and looked across the room to meet each and everyone's eyes. "We, the people of Acuna, are dedicated to peace and tranquility and have always done this through mindfulness and meditation.

When we practice mindfulness, we are in the moment every moment. This creates a wider mind view so we can take in our surroundings totally and completely. A wise man once said, in your life, you must stop to smell the flowers. He was correct about that because that is a more simple definition of mindfulness. To listen to our breathing and know that we strive to awaken our inner strengths and mental, emotional, and physical development. With mindfulness and mindful meditation, every moment is special. When we meditate, we travel within to and explore our sensations of all things around us. We feel the workings of our emotions and know that we are achieving the highest pinnacle of peace in the abundance of life.

In our mindfulness, we form an awareness that rises through our paying attention to all of our sensations, and suspending judgment of others. We allow our natural curiosity to experience the wonders of the workings of our minds. We do this with warmth and kindness to ourselves and others." She paused to shoot a breath and continued, "this is why we have no fights, and no crime in our town, and we are a model society for all of the world's people to follow if they only can."

Marina finished her mindful meditation speech with a smile and then asked for questions. Many of the town's occupants asked one question or another, but the highlight of the event was when little Pepita stood up and said quite clearly, "I have a suggestion! "

All eyes turned to the little girl who had never experienced this new information before and wondered what the child had in mind. Then, Pepita spoke with a clear and loud voice. She spoke with the words of an old soul. She spoke with the intention and mindfulness of an older person and said, "I would like to teach a class like this to my children and peers. I feel that I am perfectly suited to do this because my honorable Mother and Father have already taught me much of this information. I just didn't know that I knew it until I heard it from you, Marina. After all, the children are the future, are they not?" Everyone in the church sprang to their feet and applauded the little girl with a mindful idea. There were cheers, and great joy filled the church.

Marina just watched and listened as to do so was her strength. When the crowd had become calm once again, she spoke. "My dear little Pepita. That is a splendid idea, and I support it wholeheartedly. I will set you up with the materials you need, and you can use this holy hall for your classes. They shall be held on the first Sunday of each month, and you shall receive compensation for your hard work." The crowd applauded again, and everyone was happy and in favor of the new plan.

Then, Pepita was the only one left still standing. The room became quiet, and she spoke up again. "Um... Marina," she asked, "what is compensation?" A burst of gentle laughter filled the church, but Marina gestured for them to quiet down and tapped her podium.

"Compensation, my dear Pepita, is a payment for services or goods. You will be paid for teaching the class." And with that, Pepita sprang forward and ran up onto the stage to hug the big Monarch. Marina spread her colorful wings in full array and hugged little Pepita in a love seldom found outside of Acuna's bounds.

In the end, Pepita and Pablo stood outside in the midday sun chatting, and Pepita told her new little friend that she was going to buy a brand-new party dress with the money she earned teaching the children mindful meditation.

Pepita was finally going to walk into that dress store and try on the splendor of those new dresses. She would spend an entire hour doing this if she saw fit to do so, and she would walk out the happiest girl in the world, all thanks to goodness and love.

Animals

A bear quietly emerged from his den.

He was hungry and on a hunt for some food.

All he needed was a little something sweet to make him feel just right.

He had eaten all the berries he could, and he had found all of the honey from the hives.

He was looking for something new that he could enjoy on this fine Summer day.

He clambered through the trees of the forest and down to the riverside, looking for what would satisfy his sweet tooth.

The morning sun made his fur coat look shiny and wet, but he was soft and dry.

He decided to take a bath in the river and dry off on the shore in the sunlight, pondering what he might eat for breakfast.

A sly and sneak fox wandered near the river, careful not to expose himself to the bear.

The fox was cunning and knew how to avoid confrontations with bigger animals.

Fox and bear had never gotten along and were far from being friends.

Fox was sure to stay out of Bear's way, but today, he woke up with a sweet tooth and was on the prowl looking for something to eat .

He slipped and snaked silently through the bushes and trees, careful to stay hidden and out of sight while Bear was having his bath in the river.

The fox could smell the sweet scent of something nearby, and he wanted to see what it was.

He was following his nose when out of nowhere, a loud, obnoxious and unfriendly goose landed and honked her way to the ground near the river's edge, startling Bear and forcing Fox to take cover in a bush.

The goose had been on a very long journey.

She was flying for hours and hours and day and day.

She had lost her flock and was on her way back to find them.

She had to make sure she was back up in the air soon and on her way to find her flock again.

She was just so tired from the long hours in the sky that she needed to rest and eat before she could fly again.

The last thing she needed was a confrontation with someone, but Bear, having been startled by the honking goose and loudness as she landed, set him off in a tizzy, making him splash and clamber out of the water with a growl.

"What do you think you are doing here, Goose?" the Bear grumpily asked her.

"This is my place to find rest in the morning light. If you want to take a bath, there is plenty of rivers elsewhere."

Goose honked back a reply, "How very rude!

I have been flying for hours and hours and days and days.

I will not go elsewhere. This is where I have landed, and this is where I will stay.

Mind your own business, Bear, and get out of my way."

Bear had never been confronted like this with any other creature.

Everyone knew not to bother Bear, but this Goose was quite unfriendly and was keen on making him even more grumpy.

He stood on his hind legs, taller than a man, and tried to scare her off with a growl and a snarl.

Goose ran towards him, honking and biting at his furry knees with her beak.

"Honk! Honk! Honk!"

She cried out as she defended herself.

Bear grew angrier, and he and Goose were unhappily arguing about space and boundaries while Fox watched from the bushes.

Cunning Fox saw this quarrel as an opportunity.

"While they are both distracted, I can make my way down to the river where that sweet scent is calling. I am so hungry; I have to eat soon, or I will be just as grumpy and growly and full of quarrel as those two."

Fox silently slipped through the bushes and the trees until he came closer to the scent of sweetness that had pulled him out of his burrow this morning.

He had found himself face to face with a giant honeysuckle bush that was flapping her sweet-smelling flowers in the wind.

This is what he had wanted.

This is what had woken him up from his sleep.

He was so enamored with the aroma that he had almost forgotten that just behind him, a growling Bear and a honking Goose was disagreeing.

He was on the verge of plucking a honeysuckle flower from a branch when he was caught by silence.

Fox looked over his shoulder and saw Bear and Goose staring straight at him.

He was caught honeysuckle-handed! Bear slowly growled.

Goose slowly waddled closer.

He felt like he was being backed into a corner, but why?

He hadn't done anything but scavenged for the sweet-smelling breakfast of his dreams.

Before they got two steps closer, cunning Fox through his arms up in the air.

He was smart and wise, and he would help Goose and Bear find common ground so that they could all find peace by the river and eat to their heart's content.

"Goose. Bear. I know you have been at odds this morning, but let me show you why I have come."

He turned toward the massive honeysuckle bush behind him.

"This morning I awoke to find a sweet aroma on my mind.

I followed it on the morning breeze and thought that I would find it with ease.

But what did I find as I got closer in tune to Honeysuckle's sweet aroma in June?

A Bear and a Goose who were fighting a duel over what I can't imagine, but it's no reason to be cruel.

There is space for us all, and we are all here to eat- to relax and find harmony and to have a sweet treat.

So, what if we all had breakfast together?

We are not all alike; we are not birds of a feather.

But we can find common ground over what we all hold dear: a place to call home, to find rest, and to share.

So, what do you say?

Will you breakfast with me?

Come over here to this honeysuckle tree..."

Goose looked at Bear.

Bear looked at Goose.

They looked back at Fox and caught the scent of the sweet honeysuckle waving to them from the branches.

"Well, I suppose that would be fair, and we could all learn to share.

I see what you mean, Fox, we all need to care...about each other as equals who eat, sleep, and live, by this river, in these trees.

I am ready to give."

Bear came down from his hind legs and walked on all fours close to Fox and the honeysuckle bush.

They smiled at each other, and Bear sat down to begin his breakfast feast.

"What about you?" Fox asked of Goose.

"Will you join us for a sweet snack from the honeysuckle bush?"

Goose looked bewildered by this thoughtful idea.

In flights from North to the South and back again, she never met such a thoughtful Fox or such an affable Bear.

Bear was not growling.

He had seen reason so fast.

Maybe all he wanted was a friendship that could last.

"I confess, I am amazed that you are so thoughtful and kind.

I've never met a Fox like you or your kind.

I've never been friends with anyone but Geese.

We are all here to eat, rest, and find a little peace.

I am happy to stop fighting over something so trite.

I will join for breakfast and let go of the fight."

Goose waddled over to the giant honeysuckle bush and squeezed her way between Fox and Bear.

The 3 of them ate to their heart's content the delicious and sweet-smelling blossoms of the honeysuckle shrub.

They were bathed in the morning light as it became warmer, and by the end of their shared meal, they had already become good friends.

"Thank you, Fox, for your wisdom today.

Sometimes people fight over nothing, sometimes all day.

We all wanted the same thing- sweet foods and rest.

I will never forget you or this breakfast.

It was simply the best."

Bear was happy to have new friends and was thankful for the gift Fox had shared by using his head to solve a problem and find common ground.

"I agree with Bear, and I want to say too, that all I have ever wanted is friends like you.

Even though we are different and have different ways, we can come together and have a community that stays."

Goose was feeling more thoughtful and pleased than ever.

Soon she would have to go find her flock in the skies or on the ground nearby, but she felt glad to know she could always come here and have a fine meal with her new friends and community.

"It's my pleasure, you know, to be cunning and clever.

I want us to be happy together, no matter the weather."

Fox smiled and prepared to return to his den.

"Now that I have eaten, it's time for a rest.

I'm off to my den to have a best sleep."

"Same here!" called out Bear.

"A nap would be great!"

And Goose found herself want to delay finding her flock so she could rest by the riverbank .

"I agree with you both and will rest by the shore.

Meet back in an hour, and then we can have some more?"

She glanced at the honeysuckle, and the three of them smiled.

They knew they would find common ground by the honeysuckle again and find more than just food, but also a friend.

So off they all went to their places of rest, to find comfort and peace and the best sleep.

May you enjoy your peacefulness and rest tonight and Sweet Dreams!

His Spade

A farmer had been involved in digging in the ground of his vineyard. Then one day, when arriving back at work, he realized that his spade had gone missing. He worried that the spade just may have been taken by one of his laborers, so he interrogated them all very thoroughly. Each of the laborers said the same thing. None of them told him that it was he that had stolen the farmer's spade, so it remained a mystery.

The farmer was suspicious of their denials and therefore asserted that they must go into the town and take a pledge in a shrine that they weren't guilty of the burglary. It was because he had no boundless belief of the simple nation deities, but believed that the burglar wouldn't pass unnoticed by the town's shrewder deities.

The first thing they got inside the gates, the city crier proclaimed a reward for details regarding the burglar who took something at the shrine of the city. "Well," the Man said to himself, "it strikes me. I had better go back home again.

If these town gods can't detect the thieves who steal from their shrines, it's scarcely likely they can tell me who stole my Spade."

Zoe the Zebra

Zoe was preparing for her very first outdoor school weekend. She was reading all the information her Outdoor school leader gave them about where they were going and what they were going to do.

She came across the rules section of the book and the rule was,

1. Stay together

Zoe thought since 15 girls were going that should be easy. Then she saw the 2nd rule,

2. If you get lost. don't walk around stay where you are, we will find you.

Zoe didn't like the idea of just being lost, but she said, "If I stay with the group, I won't get lost and I won't have anyone find me."

She finished packing her bags and she headed out to tell her mom she was ready to go.

"You have everything? Sleeping bag? Warm clothes? Extra socks?" Mother persisted with a long list of everything Zoe should have in her bag.

"Yes, I have EVERYTHING," Zoes replied rolling her eyes.

They headed to the meeting point. There were already a lot of girls there. They all had their bags lined up by the bus and were wearing nametags. Zoe got out of the car and took her bag to the line and checked in. She was given a nametag and a whistle.

"What's the whistle for?" She asked

"In case you get lost. Rule #2- Stay put. We give you the whistle to blow so we can hear where you are and get to you faster if you get lost." The leader of the outdoor camp said with a smile.

Zoe walked away looking at her whistle and mumbled under her breath, "I won't need this – I am NOT getting lost!"

The girls loaded up on the bus and waved good-bye to the family standing on the curb waving.

"Okay, our door campers, " the Leader said from the front of the bus, "this is your outdoor camp weekend, and we are excited you are all here. Please make sure you wear your name badge and whistle at all times. All times girls no exceptions."

They finally arrived at the camp and everyone piled out of the bus, got their bags and set up their tents. The first evening was quiet with a bonfire, roasting marshmallows and learning who everyone was. They learned what the plan was for in the morning and they all headed off to bed.

The next day started as early as the sun was up. Breakfast on the open fire and hot cocoa to warm them up from the early morning chill.

"Today girls we are going to be going on an insect adventure," The leader announced. "we will be scouting for and documenting different insects at the camp. So when you finish breakfast we can go."

The girls headed out and started looking for insects. Each girl was instructed to locate 3 different types of insects. They all spread out and began the search. Zoe headed out behind her tent to see what she could find.

Right away she found 2 insects she had never seen before. She wrote as much as she could about them and was so excited to find her 3rd that she didn't pay attention to the fact that she had walked farther away from the group than anyone else and now she couldn't see anyone anymore. She looked around and walked back a few steps but still nothing. She began to get scared.

"Oh no, I got lost," She cried. I need to get back to the group I don't want to be here alone."

She started to head back the way she came. Or so she thought. Nothing looked familiar and she didn't remember walking by a stream. She was wondering around getting more lost. Just then she remembered Rule #2- Stay Put. Zoe found a tree to sit under and she put her backpack on the ground to sit on and wait.

She began to cry and wonder if they would come find her. She reached into her pocket to get a tissue and pulled out the whistle.

"Oh yes, if I blow the whistle they will hear where I am and come get me!' Zoe said excitedly and she began to blow the whistle as hard as she could.

"Zoeeee!" she heard someone call in the distance. "Zooooeeee!" She started to get excited and blew the whistle more.

Just then 2 rangers of the camp came around the corner and found Zoe. She jumped up and hugged them both very hard. She picked up her backpack and they took her to the rest of the group.

"Zoe we were so worried about you," another camper said.

"Yeah, we didn't know where you were." Said another

"Remembered Rule 2-Stay put!" She remarked to the group. "That is why you found me- I stayed put."

Zoe felt good that everyone missed her and was glad she was safe. If she had kept walking around, they might have taken a long time to find her, which would have been scary. She was very glad that she remembered rule #2-Stay Put.

Unicorns

There was a herd of unicorns that liked to play in an open field. They would scamper around, whinny, and sometimes play with their horns!

In this herd, there was one unicorn who was younger than the others. Her name was Rosy. The older unicorns didn't want Rosy to play with them. They said she was too small to play with them and Rosy was very sad about that because she wanted to play.

One day, Rosy the unicorn wandered off into another field where there was a farm. At the farm, Rosy saw a little girl, all by herself. And she looked sad too. The little girl didn't see Rosy. Unicorns are invisible to people. But not always.

Rosy decided to make the little girl see herself. She went to the little girl and nudged her with its horn. And suddenly, the little girl saw Rosy, a unicorn with a shiny white coat standing before her.

"Oh, what a wonderful animal you are," said the little girl. "What is your name?" she asked. The unicorn said, "Rosy, my name is Rosy." "No, that cannot be," the little girl said. "That's my name too. I'm Rosy too! Will you play with me, Rosy the unicorn?"

"Of course, I'll play with you, Rosy the little girl," said the Unicorn. "We both have the same name!" And the two played and laughed and played and laughed all day long.

When it was getting dark, Rosy's mom came out to get her for dinner. Rosy asked her mom if Rosy the unicorn could come and have dinner with them. The mother looked around and saw nothing. To her, the unicorn was invisible. "Silly girl," she said, "there's no unicorn here. Now come inside and eat."

Rosy the unicorn then went to the little girl's mother and nudged her with its horn. Suddenly, the mother saw Rosy the unicorn before her. "What a beautiful animal you are," said the mother. "Please come and have dinner with us tonight."

And Rosy the unicorn, Rosy and her mother went inside and had dinner. After, they laughed and played all through the night.

Your imagination is often your very best friend.

The Poodle and the Donkey

A boy had a little poodle, and it was his best friend. He liked to pet its fluffy white fur that was very soft. The boy took the poodle for walks. The poodle would bark and they would play. Sometimes the boy would give the poodle a special treat, food from his dinner!

One day a donkey was walking by and he looked into the window where they lived. He wanted to be petted and played with like the poodle.

"Maybe the boy will make me his pet," said the donkey.

"After all, I work all day long, and the poodle doesn't do anything. It isn't fair."

The donkey said, "If I do what the dog does, the boy may make a pet of me."

The donkey went into the house and it tried to bark, but only brayed loud. The donkey wagged its tail and knocked over a lamp and rubbed against the donkey. He hoped the boy would pet him.

But the boy became very frightened. The donkey was very big and he thought it was crazy. The boy screamed as obnoxious as he could, "Help! Help!" His father came running in and they both yelled at the donkey until it ran out of the house.

The donkey was very sad. He said, "I did what the dog did, and they screamed and chased me away. It is not fair."

Always be yourself.

The Black and White Kitten

Once upon a time, a little kitten came into this world. The kitten had many sisters and brothers. Some were gray and several were black. But this particular kitten was both white and black.

When they went to the playground to play, the kitten's brothers and sisters wouldn't play with this kitten. And sometimes they teased the kitten. They would say, you're not white, and you're not black. What are you? Are you even a cat?

And the kitten would be very sad. "Am I even a cat?" he asked himself.

One day the little kitten left his brothers and sisters by the playground. He went to the stream to get a drink and to play by himself. He was a lonely kitten but his brothers and sisters would not laugh at him when he went to the stream.

When the little kitten was at the stream, he saw a family of ducks in the water. All the baby ducklings were swimming in a line behind their mother. When they saw the little kitten drinking, they said, "come play with us, we're swimming in a line."

"I don't know if I know how to swim," the little black and white kitten said. "What will happen if I can't?"

The little ducks said, "you're silly, all little ducklings know how to swim. Come in."

The little black and white kitten went into the water and found he could swim with all the little ducks. He swam with them in a line. Until the mother duck stopped and swam back to him. "Who are you? she asked. "You don't look like a duckling.

"I'm a black and white kitten and my brothers and sisters won't play with me," said the kitten.

The Mother duck thought for a moment and said, "well, now you're a black and white duckling. You can play here anytime you like."

And all the ducklings cheered.

It's not how people look, but how they act that's important.

Mr. West

Bo West was born in a Chicago suburb and loved cars from the moment he was born. His Dad was a Gulf Station owner and operator in town, and Bo often went to work with him even before he could walk. Mr. West had a secretary who had her own secondary office adjacent to Mr. West's office. That being the case, on the days he brought his son to work with him, he paid his secretary a little more each month to watch baby Bo while he performed his mechanic and customer service work. So, to say that Bo grew up around cars was no understatement.

That was back in 1953, and in those days, cars were built strong and tough. They were meant to last, and it showed. Bo loved them! His happy childhood was now a memory, and he had children of his own. Wouldn't you know it, two boys! On the evening of his 28th. birthday, Bo, and his family went to an amusement park and had a blast. They rode the Tilt-A-Whirl, and ate Cotton Candy, and even rode the big red Ferris Wheel. The evening was becoming late, and they had wandered into the Fun House and Freak Show area. His sons wanted to go through the Fun House by themselves, and Bo thought that was fine. After the boys left, Bo and his wife caught the eye of an Arcade Operator dressed very strangely. He had on dark blue pants with large silver stars, a bright velvet purple vest and a shirt that almost hurt your eyes. It was a glimmering red and seemed to shoot out bolts of light when you looked straight at it.

The man called out to them. Bo looked at his wife, and she nodded okay, so they shuffled over to his booth. To his surprise, the man didn't offer him a game for a quarter or anything like that but instead, he beckoned him closer with his long slender finger and spoke quietly into his ear. "I know things," he whispered. "I know you love cars, and I know your Daddy took you to his Gulf Station when you were a baby." Bo almost jumped back away from the man, but something made him stay. "Okay," Bo said. "You have my attention." "Good," said the man. "My name is Clyde Fish, and I am 243 years old." At that point, Bo did step back one step and asked Clyde a key question. "What year were you born, and which two colonies were established that year?" Bo snapped. "And I want a quick answer!" he told the man. "1737, New Hampshire and Massachusetts." Clyde quickly answered with a straight-up stance. Bo was amazed, and Clyde was amused.

By that time, Bo had noticed that his wife was no longer standing next to him and had wandered back over to the Fun House to wait for her boys. Bo looked at Clyde, and Clyde stared right back into these eyes. Both men were history buffs, so both were able to quickly interact in the confirmation questions Bo had fired at Clyde. "Look, I've got to go soon and collect my family. It's getting late, and the boys have school tomorrow. Before he could get another word out, Clyde was shoving a long and thin business card at him. The card was white, and Bo wondered why it was too long and too short in height and had only an address along the bottom but no phone number. When he held it up to his eyes, Clyde's image and a hairy woman went dancing across the card. "How could he have moving pictures on a two-dimensional piece of card stock?" Bo thought. Then he looked up, and Clyde had stepped back a pace from him. "Come to my factory tomorrow night at midnight if you want to be amazed!" Clyde said in a mystical tone. "It just might change your life." Bo was still gazing down at the card, wondering if it would come to life again. When he looked up, Clyde was gone, and another man was in his place. "Play your hand for a quarter, mister?" "C'mon then; you can't lose. Play two for a quarter then mister. Right over here!"

Bo wondered if he had really met the strange man called Clyde, and then he remembered the business card. As he sauntered back over to where his family was just getting ready to come to find him, he pulled out the odd card and looked at it again. Sure enough, the dancing figures danced again. He put in in his inside shirt pocket and quickly forgot about it for the evening.

Bo told his wife everything. She was a good woman and had no trouble believing that what he said happened did happen. What she did, however, have some difficulty with was letting him go traipsing off into the old part of Chicago, known for its dark alleys, and its shady occupants. The next evening came all too quickly, and Bo got ready to go. He dressed warmly as there was a chill in the air and said goodbye to his wife. On the way over there, he reached over and checked the contents of the glove compartment. Everything he might need was present and accounted for just in case.

As he drove his restored 1953 Studebaker Pickup deeper into the bad part of town, he noticed the street lights were all flickering. While one or maybe two flickering street lights were not any huge surprise, all of them doing it in a sequence was very odd. Then, they all went out. The place was black. No residential neighborhoods around here, so only factories and industrial buildings. He slowed down but kept looking at the numbers, and then he saw what he was looking for. A small white-painted wooden sign with several numbers painted in black. Clyde's place was one of them. The sign looked so weathered; Bo wondered if it had been here since the depression. He brought his truck to a complete stop to take in the situation. Then he noticed more arrows painted on the walls that also showed the same set of numbers, so he eased his truck into the darkened alley. Slowly, ever so slowly, he forged ahead until the buildings he had been driving between fell away, leaving him in a large open parking lot with several beautiful 1930s and 1940's cars parked up against the farthest building in the back.

He pulled his Studebaker up next to the line of old cars and got out. He was walking around the first one, an old Packard that he thought must have been worth tens of thousands of dollars and then stopped to peer in the passenger side window. The car's interior looked just like the pictures of the new cars of that era his Dad had shown to him when he was little. He had his hands cupped around his eyes to try to see the details, and when he bent back up and turned around, nearly jumped out of his skin. Clyde was standing not a foot away from him. Bo's face was so close to Clyde's that they almost touched noses.

"Hello, Mr. West," Clyde announced. "Oh, hey, you surprised me there, Clyde!' Bo exclaimed. "Please, come inside," Clyde said, turning to walk towards the old building in back. "Are these wonderful classics yours?" Bo asked as they walked together. "Yes," Clyde answered. "I just brought those back the day before yesterday." He said. "Back from where?" Bo asked. "Oh, I think you mean back from when and 1941!" Clyde dropped the bomb on Bo.

"So, you mean you've had them somewhere since 1941?" Bo said. "No, I mean, I went back to 1941, purchased them, and brought them back one by one with this," Clyde said as he opened the door to his shop. Bo followed him through the door, and there, at the other end of a huge warehouse, was a machine. "I call her "Fetch," because that's what she does best. I built her in 2185 when I was just a young man." Clyde said. "Here, have a seat, Bo," Clyde said, indicating the old looking soft-bottom chairs arrayed just inside the door. "Would you like a drink?" Clyde asked as they sat down facing each other. "I have a feeling I'm going to need one," Bo stated as the two smiled at each other. Clyde walked over to an old looking bar that was built into a wall nearby. He returned with two tall glasses filled with green liquid and ice cubes. "I'm not going to ask you," Bo said as he took the tall glass. They both relaxed quietly for a few moments sipping on their drinks, and then Clyde cleared his throat. "Before I introduce you to Fetch, I'd like to fill you in on my background," Clyde told Bo. "Yes, please do," Bo responded. "I mentioned I was 243 years old. Well, those were not consecutive years, and here is the full story. I was born, as I mentioned in the year 2185, and in my youth, I found some Earth archives showing the cars from the late 1800s. I immediately fell in love with those from the 1930s and 1940s. I especially liked the 1939 coupes. I'm sorry, I'm jumping around here a little bit. I lived in the body I was born with for just over 48 years and then had my memories, and my soul saved and placed into a new 5-year-old cloned body. This process I repeated five times, which brings me to now. So, I have effectively lived 243 years but in 5 separate cloned bodies and each time beginning again about age 4 or 5. I know you will have questions, but with your leave, please allow me to continue first.

Last year I built Fetch with parts I gathered at top-secret dumping grounds, and please don't ask me how I got into them. She is a sentient being and a time machine. She was constructed for one purpose, and that is to carry one car at a time from the early twentieth century to the present time we now occupy. When you enter her, and time travel, you return to the exact moment you left from showing no lost time. This means even if you stay in say 1935 for 2 years when you return, it will be the same moment you left from here so again, no lost time.

This brings us to our timeline and you, Bo. I knew your Father in 1953 when you were just a baby, and he had his Gulf Station. I used to hold you when you were at the station sometimes as your Father and I were quite good friends. If you were to look at some of the old photos from those old days, there are a few taken of your Father and his secretary, a couple of his mechanics and me holding a tiny baby which of course, was you. There is a bit more, but that's enough for now. Let's just drink our drinks, and you can ask your questions." Bo was speechless for a moment and then began after taking one last drink and wiping his lips on his sleeve. "Of course, I did not know about you or all of the things you just told me about yourself, but I guess my first logical question is, why did you wait so long to contact me if you knew where I lived?" "Oh, that's an easy one. I was just too busy having fun traveling back and forth with new cars." Clyde said.

"Okay," Bo continued, "but what do you do with all those cars? There were only four of them out in the lot tonight, and I don't see any in here." Bo asked. "There are more in another area of the warehouse, and oh, by the way, I like to call it a factory for some reason. And to answer your first question, I take them to auctions like the big Barret Jackson auction that all the car guys know. I'm not the only time traveler, you know, just the only one who can carry cars with me when I jump. When we finish our drinks, I'll show you the rest of my operation. I have two semi-car carriers and a complete auto shop and paint shop, but only me. I do this because although I am technically from your future, I'm just an ordinary twentieth-century car guy just like you and your Daddy." Clyde finished.

I watch old movies and auto industry newsreels and then decide which cars I want and where I have to go to get them. C'mon, let me show you around." Clyde said, as he suddenly jumped up out his chair and led the way. Bo followed him down a hallway that was plastered with old car pictures showing movie stars and rock stars with their rods and pictures of the top auto industry executives on a timeline. Then, they reached a large double door entrance. Clyde entered some numbers into a code pad on the wall, and the big doors slid open, revealing the entire operation. The doorway led through to a catwalk that was far above the shop's workings, which had several levels some of which could be seen from where they were standing. It was a hidden car guy's dream garage, and there were cars lined up on racks up on the far wall with an elaborate car lift that could electronically select any car that Clyde wanted to work on or drive on any given day.

So, it seems the only question you did not ask is why I brought you here and why I am showing you my entire operation?" Clyde stated. Then, before Bo could speak, "In a way, I consider you family. Of course, I do not have any blood relatives in this timeline, but here's the deal. I feel that there is something I can offer you that nobody else on the planet can. And that is to join me as a partner and celebrate; you go on the next acquisition adventure in Fetch. What do you think?" Clyde asked. There was more than a moment of silence, and then Bo spoke again. "I accept on one condition," Bo stated. "And that is that you come to dinner at my house tomorrow night, and no more hanging out alone over here in the motor city agreed?" "Yes, agreed my friend only remember, I look the same age as you so don't tell your wife that I held you when you were a baby, or we shall be in deep caca if you know what I mean." Both men laughed, and then Bo followed Clyde back into the foyer near the shop entrance they had used earlier. "Well, are you ready?" Clyde asked. "Ready for what?" Bo asked. "Ready to go on your first car buying adventure in whatever year you like," Clyde said. "So, you can assure me that there will be no lost time, and no matter how long I stay there, I can still get home to my loving wife and slip into our bed beside her before the morning," Bo asked. "Absolutely!" was Clyde's answer.

Clyde took Bo into his office, which was very close to the sentient machine, and they sat down to talk. Clyde behind his big oak desk and Bo in front of it. "You will, of course, need a pile of cash from whatever time you choose. I have made umpteen trips to most of the different car eras and was always careful to make trades and deals to acquire enough time correct cash for every occasion, so what's your occasion Bo, my friend?" Clyde asked. Before Bo could answer, Clyde added, "oh, and I also have the time correct wardrobes and cheat sheets of the jargon and vernacular popular to each decade." Clyde informed him. "Wow, you are quite very organized, aren't you?" Bo said.

"Well, for the entire operation to work, I have to be. It's the only way!" Clyde stated. "So, what's your timeline, and you pick the car or pickup truck"? Clyde asked. "1953," Bo said with no hesitation. "Okay, I know what you want to do, and I must warn you; if you go into your Dad's station and you are also there as a baby, you will cause a great deal of trouble in the fabric of time. You have no doubt heard the word paradox?" Clyde asked with a very serious look on his face. "Yes, I understand completely, but say I just sit across the street and watch the station for a few minutes?" "Yes," Clyde replied. "That would be no problem, but don't even get out of your car that close to the main characters, understand?" "Got it!" Bo responded with a smile on his face.

"Okay, there is one more item we need to go over. I will introduce you to Fetch and acclimate you with the way she works, but when you get there, you must make some serious mental notes as to her location so you can bring the car back and find her again. You see, when you leave the machine at the other end, she will automatically go into cloak mode. You won't be able to see her, and neither will anyone else. Also, my cloak mode means you won't find her by walking into her like a kid walking into a streetlight and clocking himself. The human body and anything else will pass right through her as though she was never there. That's the beauty of the whole thing. We can't just leave this beauty sitting out in a field for all to see; now can we, my friend?" Clyde went on.

"I have a machine called a Stereo Scope to scan the areas, say for this trip, in 1953 so I can locate a field far enough away from town but still flat enough to drive a car over to Fetch when you are ready to come home. But the one critical factor is that you must not lose Fetch. If you can't find her, you will be stuck in 1953 forever. You must understand this one-point okay?" Clyde warned again.

Clyde provided Bo with everything he would need for the trip and explained the details of Fetch's operation.

He went over everything twice for good measure, and Bo indicated that he was ready.

Bo changed into 1953 attire, looked over the notes on how to speak the jargon of the times, and then climbed into Fetch. Clyde wished him all the fun in the world and asked him if he had any last questions. Bo didn't, and the machine spun up and came to life. Bo had expected a lot of buffeting and uneasy disorientation, but one minute, he was in Clyde's shop, and the next minute, he was in a large sunny field in 1953. It was instantaneous.

He checked his gear and then thanked Fetch for the smooth ride. She answered him in a low and sultry woman's voice and told him she would be awaiting another car when he returned.

Bo looked around and saw Chicago city off in the distance. He would be in for quite a long walk, but it was a lovely day, and he didn't mind in the least. After reaching the suburbs, he found the auto row right where Clyde had told him it would be. This was the moment; this was a dream come true. Along the lot front, there were shiny new and used 1950's automobiles with prices on their windshields. $750.00, $450.00, and even one with the paint a little faded for only $200.00. Amazing! He straightened up his posture, looked down at his feet to make one last check on how he looked, and then approached the dealership.

Bo had fun making his selection and then sitting down in the showroom with the salesman and making his deal. He purchased a brand new 1953 Ford Country Sedan Wagon that was fully loaded with all the features of the day. By noon he was driving the new wagon down the driveway and out onto the boulevard.

"Just one more stop," he whispered to himself. Bo knew these streets and drove directly to his Father's station. He slowly crept up on the location and pulled over against the curb on the opposite side of the road. "This should be far enough away," he thought to himself. Then, he waited. A car came up from the other direction and turned into the station; the man looked directly at Bo as he turned in. It was his Father. Bo froze. Nothing happened, and his Dad parked in the usual spot he had always used and got out of the car. "Well, look at that handsome young man!" Bo said to himself. His Dad walked into the showroom and disappeared through a door. Then he came back out with a baby in his arms. Time stood still! Bo did not move. He could not move. This was the moment in time he would always remember. "Not a bad looking kid either," he said under his breath. By two AM, Bo slipped into bed beside his wife. She said something with a mumble, and Bo said in a whisper, "You can say that again, honey!"

That night, an owl hooted, a rabbit ran across the lawn, and the sounds of a barking dog could be heard down the street. Then quiet again. "What a day!" Bo whispered. All was good in the West household.

The End

Say Please

"Can you hear it? Can you hear the circus downtown?" Bernard yelled as he came into the house. "I want to go to the Circus!" He yelled running through the house looking for someone to take him. But no one was listening to him.

He ran into the kitchen, did not see anyone. He ran into the Garage, no one. Then into the living room just

where he saw his brother watching TV.

"Hey take me to the Circus!" Bernard Exclaimed

"No, I'm not taking you." His brother replied

"Why NOT!" Bernard stomped his feet questioning his brother.

"Well, you didn't ask me nicely." He is brother said as he got up and left the room.

Bernard was getting huffy and stomped out of the room with his arms crossed. He went to sit outside and listen to the Circus music some more. As he sat there his dad was just getting home from work and he pulled in the driveway.

"Dad, do you hear the circus music? Take me to the circus!" Bernard demanded

"Good evening to you to Bernard. Did you have a good day?" Dad said with a laugh

"Yes, I want to go to the Circus now!" Bernard kept persisting

His dad rustled his hand through Bernard's hair and said "Son, maybe you should learn to ask nicely for things and people would want to do what you want." then he walked into the house.

Bernard was getting very frustrated. He wanted to go to the Circus. He didn't understand why no one would take him. After all, he did ask more than one time .

Bernard began to walk around the back yard trying to think of who could take him to the Circus. The last person to ask would his mom and he was not home yet from work. Bernard sat on the front porch steps waiting for her to come home.

Dad called out to Bernard, "Dinner is ready Bernard, please come wash your hands for dinner."

"I want to go to the Circus," Bernard said again as he walked back into the house.

Just as he was sitting down for dinner his mom came through the front door and Bernard burst up from the table waving his arms, "Mom, Mom the Circus is here. Take me to the circus."

"Well hello to you to Bernard. It's been a long day so please stop yelling and let's go eat dinner." Mom said patiently as she directed him back to the table.

"But the Circus…" Bernard tried again

"Bernard Please, let's eat dinner." Mom said and smiled

As the family sat and ate dinner they talked about their day and what exciting things had happened at school and work.

"Please pass the potatoes," Dad asked Bernard

"Please pass the Roast," Mom Asked Bernard

"Please hand me a napkin." Asked his brothe r

Bernard kept passing things along and realized that each time they asked him for something they said….please. He sat for a moment and asked, "Why do you always please when you ask me for something?"

"It's polite and if you learn to ask for things nicely you are more likely to get what you want." His dad replied as he added a scoop of potatoes to his plate.

"That is correct, Bernard, barking orders at people is rude and makes people not want to listen to what you ask." Mom chimed in. "Please finish your food son your father made such a great dinner."

Bernard finished his dinner and asked, "May I please to from the table?"

Everyone laughed and Mom replied, "Yes Bernard you may be excused."

Bernard went up to his room to do his homework and thought about all of the 'Pleases' that went around the dinner table. He wondered if he has asked nicely and said please about going to the circus if he would have been able to go. He finished his homework and get ready for bed .

Bernard woke up early with the Sunrise and opened his window to listen if he could still hear the Circus. But he heard nothing. He was sad. After all, he thought he had missed his chance to go because he didn't say please. He got dressed and went down for breakfast. He sat at the table with his eyes looking out the window dreaming of what the circus might be like. Lions jumping, elephants dancing, Clowns twirling on balls...his thoughts were running away on the wonderful things he missed out on because he didn't say please.

The day went on and the family decided to go into town for the afternoon. At one moment Bernard popped his up and listened-was it- could it be- the Circus was still in town. He wanted to go more now than before and as he turned to his mom to ask one more time, he remembered that he had been rude and demanding the day before and no one wanted to take him so this time he was determined to be polite and say please when he asked.

"Mom! Dad! Can we go to the circus today, pleeeease?" Bernard looked up the parents of his with his hands folded in front of him. His parents looked at one another and smiled.

"Bernard, it looks as you've learned an invaluable lesson. It's essential to be polite and please when asking for things instead of demanding folks to do things. Today, because you have remembered to ask properly, yes, we can go to the Circus. Thank you for asking politely." His father replied

Bernard jumped up and down with excitement and thanked his parents for taking him to the Circus. He got to watch Lions, Elephants, and Clowns. He even got some Cotton Candy.

From that day on Bernard tried hard to remember to say please when he was asking for something. He wanted to be polite. Most of the time he got what he was asking for so he was glad he learned to say Please.

Charlie The Cheetah Chews with Her Mouth Open

Chomp, Crunch, Munch....Charlie Cheetah was enjoying her lunch at a picnic with friends on a sunny Saturday afternoon.

Chomp, Crunch, Munch....Charlie Cheetah laughed as she ate her lunch spitting food on the picnic blanket. Her friends were not very happy with her and they got up and moved away from her to eat their lunch.

"What's wrong?" Charlie asked

"Charlie, we don't want to eat the food that's been in your mouth. You keep spitting it all over." One of her friends said

"I do?" Charlie replied. She seemed confused as she took another bite of lunch… Chomp, Crunch, Munch.

The next morning was Sunday and Charlie's family headed off to Church. After Church, her family always went out for dinner. Her favorite place was the buffet. She could eat all she wanted and could have whatever she wanted. Charlie was looking forward to going out to eat .

Once she got to the Buffet, she loaded up her plate with so many delicious things she couldn't wait to get to the table to start eating. Chomp, Crunch, Munch she began taking bites of this and bites of that, Chomp, Crunch, Munch. Her sister looked over at her and gave her a weird look.

"Why are you spitting food on the table all the time? It's gross!" her sister said

"What do you mean I am not spitting food out." Charlie looked confused as ignored her sister and took a few more bites- Chomp, Crunch, Munch.

Monday came and off to School Charlie went. She had packed her lunch today and she was proud of her meal. She couldn't wait for lunch to come. She had packed a peanut butter and banana sandwich, some BBQ chips, a few carrots, and a juice box. "What a meal." She thought to herself. It will be delicious!

When lunch came Charlie got out her lunch box and began to eat. Chomp, Crunch, Munch, Chomp, Crunch, Munch. One by one the other students began to leave the table or scoot away from Charlie. At first, she didn't notice but halfway through lunch, she found herself sitting alone at the table. She looked around and saw that there was a mess of food on the table. Chewed up food .

"Gross!" she said out loud. "Someone forgot to clean this table before lunch and no one wants to sit here."

Later that evening Charlie offered to help make dinner. She set the table and also made everybody that is sure had a plate, knives, forks, and drinking glass. They passed the food around and said grace before eating. Then Chomp, Crunch, Munch it began.

Charlie began eating her food and spitting it out all over the table. Her family sat and watched for a while and her mother finally spoke up. "Charlie what is going on?" why are you chewing with your mouth open? You are spitting food all over the table honey."

"I am?" Charlie replied, "I always eat this way."

Then Charlie remembered the picnic on Saturday when her friends said she was spitting food all over the picnic blanket and moved away from her because they didn't want her chewed up food in their meals. Then she remembered the Buffet and her sister making a weird face about how she was spitting food. Then at that moment at dinner, she looked at the table and saw her chewed up food on the table cloth.

"Is that from me?" She asked

"Yes" her mother replied. "You have a habit of eating with your mouth open and that spits food all over when you eat. "

Charlie sat there for a minute and thought about it. She did chew with her mouth open and there were a lot of times people had said something but she just didn't get it. Today she finally understood.

"I am sorry for chewing with my mouth open. I didn't know all that food was from me. I wouldn't like that either. I will try hard to remember to chew with my mouth closed from now on." Charlie said with her hands on her hips and in a strong voice.

The next day Charlie made her lunch again and headed off to school. At lunch, the other students watched to see if they would be ok sitting next to Charlie they didn't want to hear or see Chomp, Crunch, Munch. But today they heard... nothing. Charlie was chewing with her mouth closed and no food was spitting out of her mouth. The other students were relieved and moved over to sit with Charlie.

It was a hard thing to remember sometimes but Charlie tried hard to chew with her mouth closed at every meal. No more food spitting out on the table, no more weird looks from her sister and she enjoyed sitting and eating with her friends once again. "Chewing with your mouth closed is important." Charlie thought. "I wish I knew that sooner!"

The Raven and the Crow

A quite a while before, in a land brimming with knights and breathtaking damsels, there existed a wicked king. He hated everyone and also never had a great day. The king lived in a big castle, and there were many spires all around over the great wall which surrounded the king's domain name. The spires had been built high into the skies and then seemed to go on forever and in those existed a solitary raven.

There was a very long road that led to the king's castle, and if you wanted to go to the caste, you had to pass through the dark forest. There was no other way you see as the road went through that dark forest, and that was the only road there was. In the forest, many crows were living high up in the trees. The crows were always very busy, and they were thought to be the smartest birds in the kingdom.

One day, the raven flew out of his high spire and made the trip into the dark forest. He flew high and fast until he reached just about the center of the forest near where the road passed through it. He landed on the greatest department of probably the tallest tree he might get and sat there resting. Next, he took flight once more and dove correctly printed near the road searching for the crows he'd heard about that were supposed to be very smart. Soon, the raven found where crows had been searching for winter foods to stash away once the ice came and covered the ground. This made it challenging but not impossible to locate the bugs they liked eating every single day.

When the crows saw the raven, they all stopped their foraging and sat still, staring at him. Then the biggest crow stepped up and spoke to the raven. "Hello there, Mr. Raven. To what do we owe this honor. I know that you live in the tallest castle spire, and you serve the king, so why have you left the safety of the kingdom to come into the dark forest?" he asked. "I have come to find you, so I may ask a question." The raven said. "Well, you have found me, so go on, ask away." The large crow said.

"The king is always irritable and cross with everyone in the castle, and he doesn't have a wife, Uh, I mean a queen." The raven told him. I have tried singing to him, I have brought him gifts which I made with my own two claws, and I have made many suggestions, but nothing is working, and so that is why I came to see you oh kindly crow." The raven said. "Hmmm," said the big crow. "I think we might need some time to think this over, don't you?" he asked the raven. "Yes, let us have food and drinks." The crow said to the raven. "After our tummies are full, perhaps an idea will alight upon us."

All the crows followed the big crow and the raven into the big hollow tree they liked to use for thinking. In the hollow, all the birds sat down around a very long table and pulled up their chairs to talk. They talked of the weather, talked of the forest and the castle, and finally talked of the irritable king. Only when they started to question if they'd be in a position to assist the king, among the newer crows way down after the kitchen table nurtured his wing and had a thing to say. Yes, sonny, what's it? the fundamental crow asked. Well, does the king learn how to meditate? minor sonny crow asked. To the great surprise of his, everyone around the huge table smiled at him and also made excited and happy noises.

Being young and excitable, little sonny crow spoke up again. "I think if the king knew how to meditate, then he would know how to be mindful, and if he knew how to be mindful, then he would have already attracted a proper queen," Sonny said. "I believe you're right!" stated the raven getting much more thrilled by the moment. "But how can we teach him?" the important crow asked. "We cannot just fly from and explain to him he has got it all wrong and also understand the best way to address him? Can we?" he requested, exploring the raven.

The raven was quiet for the moment. Then, he said, "I know, let's just ask him if he's thought about meditation, and that way, he'll say that of course, he has because you know he always thinks he is right and he always thinks that he knows everything. Then, we will have planted the seed in the king's mind to ask for help. And we won't have to sound like we are telling him anything. Kings don't like to be told what to do, you know." The raven stated .

"All right then," the big crow said, "Suppose you tell us what we can do to help Mr. Raven." He said. "Well," the raven said, "you could all fly with me to the castle, and we'll all talk to him together. You all meditate, don't you?" he asked the group. "Oh yes," and "Of course," and "we sure do!" kinds of sounds were heard all around the table as though none of the crows wanted to be known as no nothings who did not know how to meditate. Then there was a lot of scuffling of feet and shuffling legs under the table as things became settled. "All right then," the raven said. "We are all off to the caste!"

The band of birds followed the royal raven out of the hollow, and when they were all out there together again, the raven said, "we fly in formation! Follow me, boys!" and they were off. They flew up and out of the forest and far above the canopy. They flew in proper formation as the raven had instructed, and they arrived at the castle just like that. A proper formation is the right thing for birds who are flying together to do.

They all followed the raven down and down and watched as he landed on a landing on the top tier of the corner spire. When all the birds were down, the raven turned to them and said, "follow me to my home here in the corner spire, and we'll get ready to see the king." They all followed him again as instructed, and they filed into his home there in the spire. "Everybody have a seat, and I will make us all some nice Mint Tea." The raven said to the group. "Mint Tea is good for the mind, you know." He informed them. Mint Tea is good for mindfulness and meditation, he informed them. There seemed to be a collective Ah, throughout, along with soon, they were all consuming the Mint Tea. Next, the raven informed them that he will need to head to the king's chamber to find out what sort of spirits he was in then come to gather them. Only then could they almost all go well to watch the king.

The raven left them all as well as went on the royal chamber to see the king. The king was relaxing in his great soft bottom chair in front of a roaring flame poking separate at it with the poker of his. When the raven arrived in, he did gradually and thoroughly as was connecting when someone approached a king. The lord of mine, he stated softly. May I've the honor of talking with you, your highness? the raven asked. Oh, it is you raven, the king stated, flipping in his seat to determine who it was. Yes yes do are available in. I will welcome a little organization as it's boring and lonely being a king alone, you realize, the king informed him.

Indeed, I assume it will be the highness of yours, but it is exactly what I came to view you about sire! he announced. What is that you simply mention then? the king questioned. Well sire, I've brought several buddies coming from the forest with me, and also I'd love to ask for that you simply let them join us, and also we are going to explain the ideas of ours for you sire, that's, in case you do not care about excessive sire, the instantly nervous raven said.

"Oh, by all means, go and fetch them and perhaps we can all sit together around my fire here and roast things to eat? Would you like that, raven?" the king asked. "Oh yes,, sire, that is a splendid idea. I always count on you to come up with splendid ideas, and there, you've done it again. You are a good and wise king." The raven told him. "Never mind that raven, go and fetch your friends and I will be right here waiting for you to return with them, now go!" the king said, making a shooing motion with his hand.

The raven was very happy that the king was in an unusually good mood indeed and hurried back to his home in the spire to get the others. When he arrived, all the crows were in a bantering conversation about what they thought the king needed. One said he needed a vacation. Another said he needed a new horse to ride around the countryside and yet another said that he needed a queen. The raven heard that and broke in, "Yes," the raven said, "He needs a queen all right, and that's exactly what we are going to get him if we have to go door to door in the town searching for her ourselves."

"Say," another small crow said, "I think you've hit on a very good idea. If we search the town and tell everyone that the kink is searching for a queen, which would be a great thing," he said. Then another of the smaller crows chimed in and said, "Hey, why not put up posters all around the town that tell they, people, that the king is searching for a queen. I do believe that would work, you know." He shrieked.

"Okay," the raven said, "that's enough ideas for now, the king is waiting for us, and we must go to his highness now!" the raven announced. Everyone got up and ruffled their feathers so that they were all to see the king, and they filed out of the ravens home, again following him, and marched over to the king's chamber. When they got there, the raven told them in a whisper, "now everyone be courteous and mindful when in the king's presence. He is, after all, the king. And don't everyone talk at the same time. We must have order in the king's chamber, or he will become irritated again, and believe me, you do not want that!"

Everyone shook their heads yes in agreement, and in they all went. "Ah raven, you have brought your friends from the forest. Good, good, very good!" he said with a big smile on his kingly face. "Find seats, everyone, and let us begin to talk and enjoy ourselves." The king told them. Soon, the raven began by saying to the king, "Sire, do you practice mindfulness and meditation?" He then waited for the king's response. "Why yes, err, ahh, no, actually I do not. I know the practice and have been meaning to start such a thing, but at this time, no, I have yet to explore mindfulness and meditation. I have heard very good things about it, though." The king told them.

"We is pleased to enable you to obtain started," the raven told the king. "We are good at deep breathing and will teach you all the things you have to learn about it." The raven stated to the king. "Is which right?" the king asked. "Well, then allow us not waste some much more time. We begin appropriate now!" the king commanded. All of the crows took turns, informing the king everything they knew about how you can get going in meditation, after which the raven spoke up once again.

"Sire, if you are going to keep up the meditation of yours and practice mindfulness, you'll undoubtedly have a feeling of friendliness and an innovative sense of appeal to the presence." He told the king. "And then there's a high probability you'll quickly possess a queen flooring the throne of her by your side to support you rule over your domain."

"We are going to help you find your queen sire," a small crow in the back chimed in. "Ah, I think a lot of you all, and I don't think I tell you that enough." The king said. "I don't think I tell anyone that at all." All the birds scuffed their shoes and looked down at their feet. Then the raven spoke up. "My lord," he began, we will find you a queen, and you will be happy very soon, and your new queen will love you, sire!" the raven said.

And from that time forward, the king was happy because he knew now that those around him could love him. "I just never knew what love felt!" the king said to the birds around him. Then, all the crows and the raven lined up and shook the king's hand and even hugged the unlikely king.

"From now on," the king said, "I will be more mindful of those around me, and I will never be wicked again. I was wrong to ever be that way when I could have chosen to be loved and to love others who I know love me." That was the day that the king became known as the loving and caring king, and never again did anyone ever call him a wicked king.

Always be mindful of others!

Alligators

Have you ever seen an alligator with a cat on its back?

It's not every day you will see such a sight, especially when it swims by in the middle of the night.

This story is one that you'll just have to hear, as you snuggle in deep to your covers for sleep.

So, without further ado, lie back on your bed, close your eyes, and rest your head.

Take a deeeep breath in, let it out smooth, and discover what happens with the cat and the alligator under the moon.

There are plenty of creatures that live down in the swamp, and many of them are just as curious as strange as some you might find in the sea.

Take the alligator for instance.

Close your eyes and imagine what an alligator looks like.

Long tail, long snout, flat head, long body, short, little legs.

Alligators love to coast along the waters of the swamp, the rivers and the lakes, only their eyes and the ridges of their backs sticking out of the water.

One night, just such an alligator who doing just such a thing was under the moon, drowsily coasting along in the swamp.

The bullfrogs were croaking, the cicadas were humming, and the fireflies were asleep for the night.

The alligator calmly and quietly swept through the swamp, the moonlight shining down.

It was almost difficult to tell she was even swimming there, for she looked like a floating log and nothing much more than that.

It was something she was good at, the alligator in the swamp, just coasting along, hidden from sight, body underwater, and until...chomp! Chomp! CHOMP!

She would leap out of the water, snatch her dinner, roll and twist, and turn her body in the water.

All the animals in the swamp new to keep a watchful eye, for the alligator was easy to miss as she hid beneath the water, not unlike a cat, who quietly stalks its prey and has impeccable instincts.

Just such a cat was hunting by a tree near the swamp and was almost about to grab her tasty mouse dinner when out of the swamp leaped the alligator who was hungrier than a hippopotamus.

"Yeeeeeooooowww!" Meowed the cat.

She was startled and leaped up into the tree, her tasty mouse dinner scrambling away.

The alligator was unhappy to have lost her catch, the cat who was quick and able to get away, but she wanted to get at her anyway.

The alligator stayed on the bank of the swamp and waited up in the tree for the cat to come down eventually.

The cat saw what the alligator had in mind and quickly reminded herself that she was a cat and that there was nothing to be afraid of.

Didn't she have claws and sharp teeth, too?

Wasn't she just as fast and good at catching things?

She didn't want to be anybody's dinner so she worked her way down the tree and did something no other creature in the swamp had ever done before.

As you may have already learned, cats always land on their feet, even from two stories high!

The cat leaped from the tree and right onto the alligators back, and since alligators have very short arms and legs, well...there was nothing the alligator could do except jump back in the water.

And as you may have already learned, cats don't like getting wet, so when they alligator jumped back in the swamp and began to twirl around like a spinning log, the cat had to run in place on top of the spinning alligator to stay dry.

Can you even imagine it?

Close your eyes and picture it now: a peaceful swamp under the pale moonlight and a silly alligator rolling her body over and over again while a cat skitters on top of her to stay out of the water, like running on a barrel or a log.

The cat realized that this could go on forever, so she knew she had to stop it.

As you may have already learned, cats are masters in the art of Zen, and this cat wasn't about to let a twirling alligator disrupt her normal state of cat-calm.

The cat knew that to stop the alligator from her twirling frenzy, she would have to do something a little out of character.

She decided to stick her claws into the alligators back and let herself get soaking wet with swamp water.

It was the only way to make a change in the situation and move forward.

The alligator felt those sharp, pointy claws dig in, and she stopped spinning immediately, returning to her resting alligator pose.

"Ooooooooww," she commented in a long, drawn-out sigh that was as lazy as a Southern Summer, for alligators have very thick skin, and it was hardly a scratch.

But it was enough to stop her in her twirling tracks.

"Serves you right for scaring me out of my dinner, into a tree, and onto your back," the swamp-soaked cat revealed to the alligator.

"You might find that being a little more Zen will get you a better catch," the cat continued to teach.

"I beg your pardon?" the alligator was taken aback.

Never in all her days, floating in the swamp had she ever met anyone she couldn't catch or best with speed.

"I am nothing but stealth, Cat. May I remind you how scared you were by my presence?

You couldn't even tell I was coming."

"That may be true," replied the cat.

"It seems to me you have met your match.

I am just as stealthy and just as quick. You'll never dine on my kind. We are too alike."

The cat was perched on the back of the alligator who had calmly begun to float down through the swampy waters.

The cat was quite content to take a relaxing ride.

She was almost inclined to curl up and take a catnap.

"What you say is true, and so I suspect we should call each other friend."

The two creatures calmly floated through the water together and soon, they were laughing, telling jokes, and helping each other look for tasty snacks under the pale moonlight.

The cat sat on the alligators back, and they drifted deeper into the swamp, showing each other what they could do to catch a meal.

Neither of them was very good at the surprise attack, and they laughed and joked about how silly they could be.

The cat was ready to take a long nap, and as she curled up into a ball on the alligator's back, she said, "Oh me, oh my, I am ready for a nice long nap.

We have been up all night laughing and talking about life.

Do you mind, friend?

Can I take a nap on your back until the night ends?"

The alligator smiled and yawned and kept floating along.

"Sleep, friend. Rest your eyes, and take comfort on my back.

I promise not to leap out for a snack.

I think I shall do the same and float along with my eyes closed until we both wake again...or until there is something good to eat..."

They both laughed and prepared to sleep, swimming along the swamp at night, feeling the moonlight.

And what a way to become fast friends, the cat, and the alligator, together at last.

Have you ever seen an alligator with a cat on its back?

It's not every day you will see such a sight, especially when it swims by in the middle of the night.

This was a story of unlikely friendship and of learning from friends and as the cat and the alligator sleep in the swamp, may you dream of them on their adventures.

The swamp is quiet...the moon is out.

The night falls on friends sleeping soundly, a cat curled up on an alligator's back.

May you find the same peacefulness and moment of Zen, dreaming about the story of these two unlikely friends.

Sweet dreams!

www.ingramcontent.com/pod-product-compliance
Lightning Source LLC
Chambersburg PA
CBHW070936080526
44589CB00013B/1527